ALFREDO TUTUHATUNEWA

Development Of Shopee's Competitive Strategy

With A Multidimensional Scaling And SWOT Approach

Contents

Foreword

Praise and thanks be to God Almighty, for His love and inclusion, so that this Final Report on Basic Research Excellence with PNBP Funds for the Faculty of Engineering Year 2023 can be completed. In this study, the authors used the Multidimensional Scaling and SWOT approaches to formulate Shopee's e-commerce competitive strategy.

The implementation of research and the preparation of this final report cannot be separated from the help of various parties, for that, on this occasion, the author would like to express his sincere appreciation and gratitude, to:

1. The rector and vice rectors of Pattimura University;
2. Head of the Research Institute of Pattimura University Ambon and all staff;
3. Dean and Vice Deans of the Faculty of Engineering Pattimura University.
4. The Head and Secretary of the Industrial Engineering Department of the Faculty of Engineering, Unpatti, for the opportunity given so that the author received this research grant.

This research report is still full of shortcomings and limitations so that the author is happy to receive input, both in the form of suggestions and criticism to improve this Research Report.

Finally, I hope that this writing can be useful for those who need additional understanding and knowledge about supply chain management.

Abstract

E-commerce plays an important role in providing various needs of the society. Currently, various e-commerce companies operate in Indonesia. This research takes Shopee, one of the e-commerce companies operating in Indonesia, as the object of research. Shopee has become one of the leading e-commerce companies today, due to the large number of customers. This competition encourages consumers to be more careful and selective in determining which e-commerce products to choose.

The research aims to analyze the positioning of shopee against several e-commerce competitors, seen from seven attributes, namely; 1) ease of use, 2) quality of information, 3) customer service, 4) web/application design, 5) controllable process, 6) quality of results and 7) price. The method used is Multidimensional scaling (MDS), one of the multivariate techniques that is able to describe objects in perceptual maps, to show their similarity or dissimilarity with other objects, based on various selected attributes. The second objective is to develop a strategy to win the competition based on current positioning, with SWOT analysis.

The results showed that Shopee is in a different position and dimension when compared to the other 5 e-commerce on the perception map. Shopee's position is supported by the attributes of ease of use, controllable process, quality of results, website design and customer service, as Shopee's main advantages. There are two main strategies that Shopee must do if it wants to win the competition with other e-commerce, namely cooperation with seller partners to hold promotions to reduce prices, and at the same time increase cooperation and supervision to partners, to ensure the quality of information shared on the Shopee web.

Keywords: e-commerce, multidimesional scaling, perceptual map, shopee

Introduction

The Development of E-Commerce and Shopee's Positioning Strategy

The rapid advancement of technology has significantly impacted people's lives, particularly in terms of their daily needs and preferences. As the world becomes more fast-paced, individuals increasingly seek convenience and efficiency in their everyday activities. This shift in consumer behavior has paved the way for the rise of various service-providing companies, including those operating in the e-commerce sector. The business world has capitalized on these developments, leveraging the power of information and communication technology to expand their reach and cater to the evolving demands of consumers.

E-commerce, which refers to the buying and selling of goods or services through electronic media, has emerged as a game-changer in the retail industry. Companies engaging in e-commerce rely on internet access and information technology, such as electronic data interchange (EDI), to facilitate transactions. These platforms enable vendors to showcase their products and services directly to users, offering a seamless and convenient shopping experience. Gupta [2] provides a comprehensive definition of e-commerce, describing it as "the use of electronic communications and digital information processing technologies in business transactions to create, transform, and redefine relationships for value creation between or among organizations, and between organizations and individuals."

In the highly competitive e-commerce landscape, companies must continuously strive to differentiate themselves and offer unique value propositions to consumers. The success of an e-commerce platform largely depends on its ability to provide an attractive, user-friendly, and profitable sales system that benefits both the company and its customers. Therefore, companies must pay close attention to their sales systems and ensure that they align with the latest advancements in information technology.

Indonesia's e-commerce market has witnessed significant growth in recent years, with numerous players vying for market share. Among these companies is Shopee, which has established itself as a prominent player in the industry. However, the intense competition has made it imperative for Shopee to develop effective strategies to stand out from its rivals and capture the attention of consumers. To achieve this, Shopee must focus on product positioning, which involves defining its products in the minds of consumers based on key attributes and differentiating itself from competitors [3].

Positioning is a crucial aspect of a company's marketing strategy, as it helps to establish a unique identity and value proposition in the minds of consumers. According to Hiam and Schewe, as cited by Hasan [4], the process of effective positioning involves several steps. These include determining relevant product-markets, collecting data on customer needs, identifying competitors, determining evaluation standards, creating perceptual maps, identifying positioning gaps, and planning and implementing positioning strategies.

To gain a deeper understanding of consumer perceptions and preferences, Shopee can employ Multidimensional Scaling (MDS), a multivariate technique that visually maps respondents' perceptions and preferences in a geometric map [5]. This perceptual map helps to identify the dimensions that consumers most frequently use when evaluating an object, the relative importance of each dimension, and the perceptual relationships between the observed objects. By analyzing the generated perception map, Shopee can gain valuable insights into how consumers perceive its products and services in relation to those of its competitors.

Armed with this information, Shopee can then conduct a SWOT analysis to develop a competitive strategy [6]. The SWOT analysis involves identifying the company's strengths, weaknesses, opportunities, and threats, allowing it to capitalize on its strengths, address its weaknesses, seize opportunities, and mitigate potential threats. By combining the insights gained from the MDS and SWOT analysis, Shopee can develop a comprehensive positioning strategy that effectively communicates its unique value proposition to its target audience.

To further enhance its competitive edge, Shopee must also focus on continuously improving its platform's user experience, ensuring that it remains intuitive, responsive, and secure. This may involve investing in advanced technologies such as artificial intelligence and machine learning to personalize product recommendations, streamline the checkout process, and enhance customer support. Additionally, Shopee should prioritize building strong relationships with its vendors, ensuring that they have access to the tools and resources needed to succeed on the platform.

Moreover, Shopee must stay attuned to the evolving needs and preferences of its customers, adapting its strategies accordingly. This may involve conducting regular market research, analyzing customer feedback, and monitoring industry trends to identify emerging opportunities and potential disruptions. By maintaining a customer-centric approach and demonstrating agility in the face of change, Shopee can position itself for long-term success in the highly dynamic e-commerce market.

The rise of e-commerce has transformed the way businesses operate and consumers shop, creating both challenges and opportunities for companies like Shopee. To thrive in this competitive landscape, Shopee must develop a strong positioning strategy that effectively communicates its unique value proposition to its target audience. By leveraging tools such as Multidimensional Scaling and SWOT analysis, Shopee can gain valuable insights into consumer perceptions and preferences, allowing it to refine its offerings and differentiate itself from its competitors. Ultimately, by staying customer-focused, technologically advanced, and adaptable to change, Shopee can establish itself as a leader in the Indonesian e-commerce market and beyond.

Literature Review

State of the Art

The state-of-the-art in e-commerce business strategy development involves the integration of perceptual mapping and SWOT analysis. Perceptual maps, derived from multidimensional scaling (MDS) analysis, are used to visualize customer perceptions and preferences, aiding in the formulation of effective positioning strategies. This is particularly relevant in the context of e-commerce, which has experienced significant growth, especially during the COVID-19 pandemic.

E-commerce is recognized as a crucial marketing strategy in the era of globalization. However, the competitive nature of the e-commerce landscape necessitates strategic development based on a thorough understanding of customer perceptions and market dynamics. SWOT analysis, which evaluates internal strengths and weaknesses alongside external opportunities and threats, provides a comprehensive framework for assessing a company's strategic situation and addressing challenges.

By combining perceptual mapping with SWOT analysis, businesses can gain valuable insights into customer preferences, market positioning, and competitive advantages. This integrated approach enables the development of tailored e-commerce strategies that are responsive to market trends and customer needs, ultimately enhancing competitiveness and driving business growth.

E-commerce

E-commerce has revolutionized the way businesses operate and interact with their customers, offering a convenient and efficient platform for conducting transactions and exchanging goods, services, and information. The definition of e-commerce encompasses a wide range of activities, from online shopping and electronic payments to automated business processes and digital service delivery. As Kalakota and Whinston [12] highlight, e-commerce can be viewed from multiple perspectives, each emphasizing different aspects of this transformative technology.

From a communication perspective, e-commerce enables the seamless delivery of goods, services, information, and payments through digital channels such as computer networks and electronic devices. This allows businesses to reach a global audience and facilitates instant, round-the-clock transactions. The ease of communication and information exchange fostered by e-commerce has greatly enhanced the efficiency and effectiveness of business operations, enabling companies to respond quickly to customer needs and market trends.

From a business process perspective, e-commerce leverages technology to automate and streamline various aspects of business operations, such as order processing, inventory management, and customer service. By digitizing and integrating these processes, businesses can reduce costs, minimize errors, and improve overall efficiency. Automated workflows also enable companies to handle larger volumes of transactions and scale their operations more effectively, providing a competitive edge in today's fast-paced business environment.

From a service perspective, e-commerce serves as a powerful tool for enhancing customer satisfaction and loyalty. By offering a wide range of products and services online, businesses can cater to the diverse needs and preferences of their customers. E-commerce platforms also provide customers with convenient access to product information, reviews, and support, enabling them to make informed purchasing decisions. Moreover, the ability to process orders and deliver products quickly and efficiently through e-commerce channels helps businesses improve the quality of their services and meet the growing expectations of modern consumers.

From an online perspective, e-commerce has transformed the way people shop and consume information. The Internet and other online platforms have become integral parts of the modern shopping experience, allowing customers to browse, compare, and purchase products from the comfort of their homes or on the go using mobile devices. This has greatly expanded the reach of businesses, enabling them to tap into new markets and customer segments. Online marketplaces and e-commerce websites have also become important sources of product information and reviews, influencing consumer behavior and purchasing decisions.

The importance of e-commerce has become even more apparent in the wake of the COVID-19 pandemic [10]. With social distancing measures and lockdowns limiting physical store visits, many consumers have turned to online channels to fulfill their shopping needs. This has accelerated the adoption of e-commerce across various sectors, from retail and food delivery to healthcare and education. Businesses that had already invested in e-commerce infrastructure were better positioned to adapt to these changes and maintain their operations, while those that had lagged behind were forced to quickly embrace digital transformation to remain competitive.

As companies face increasing pressure to protect and expand their market share in this rapidly evolving landscape, the adoption of e-commerce technologies has become a strategic necessity [11]. By leveraging the power of e-commerce, businesses can enhance their visibility, reach new customers, and streamline their operations. However, the successful implementation of e-commerce strategies requires a deep understanding of customer needs, market trends, and technological advancements. Companies must also invest in robust e-commerce platforms, secure payment systems, and efficient logistics networks to ensure a seamless and satisfying customer experience.

E-commerce has emerged as a driving force behind the transformation of modern business practices and consumer behavior. By enabling the electronic exchange of goods, services, and information, e-commerce has opened up new opportunities for businesses to grow, innovate, and compete in the digital age. As the world continues to embrace digital technologies and online platforms, the importance of e-commerce will only continue to grow, making it a critical component of any successful business strategy.

Positioning

Positioning is defined as finding the right position in the market after determining the segmentation strategy used [13]. Meanwhile, Kasali [14], defines positioning as a form of communication strategy to enter the consumer's brain window so that the products and brands offered contain certain meanings, which in various aspects reflect the advantages of the product or brand in an associative relationship. Thus positioning is concerned with how a manufacturer positions its product or brand among competitors and positions its product with the brand in the minds of consumers or customers.

Positioning in marketing can be understood from two perspectives. First, it's the strategic process of identifying and establishing a distinct place for a product or brand within the market, especially after a specific target segment has been chosen. This involves understanding the competitive landscape and tailoring the product's image to appeal to the selected segment.

Second, positioning can be seen as a communication strategy. It's about creating a strong impression in the minds of consumers, associating the product or brand with specific meanings and values. This goes beyond just features and benefits; it's about crafting a narrative that resonates with the target audience, highlighting the unique advantages and differentiating the product from competitors. Ultimately, positioning is about shaping how consumers perceive and remember a product or brand, influencing their purchasing decisions.

Apart from using attributes as a tool for developing positioning statements, marketing practitioners can also use other means [14]:

1. Positioning based on product differences. Marketers can show their market where their products are different from competitors (unique product features). Manufacturers who produce priority products can do this method. Product differentiation positioning is a strategy where marketers emphasize the unique features or attributes that set their products apart from competitors. This approach is particularly effective for manufacturers who produce priority products, as it allows them to highlight the distinct value proposition of their offerings. By showcasing the unique product features, marketers can create a clear differentiation in the market, attracting consumers who value those specific qualities. This strategy not only helps in capturing a niche market but also in building a strong brand identity based on the product's unique selling points.

2. Positioning based on product benefits. Product benefits can also be highlighted as positioning as long as they are considered important by consumers. Benefits can be economic (cheap, reasonable, according to quality), physical (durable, good, pleasing to the eye) or emotional (related to self-image). Positioning based on product benefits is a strategy where marketers emphasize the advantages or value that consumers gain from using their products. This strategy focuses on the positive outcomes or experiences that consumers can expect when they choose a particular product. These benefits can be classified into three main categories: economic benefits, which highlight the financial advantages

of the product, such as affordability or cost savings; physical benefits, which focus on the tangible aspects of the product, such as durability, functionality, or aesthetics; and emotional benefits, which appeal to the psychological or emotional needs of consumers, such as enhancing self-esteem or social status. By effectively communicating the relevant benefits to the target audience, marketers can create a compelling value proposition that resonates with consumers and drives their purchasing decisions.

3. Positioning based on usage. The distribution that is emphasized is the use of the product. Positioning based on usage is a strategy where marketers emphasize the different ways or situations in which a product can be used. This approach aims to broaden the appeal of the product by showcasing its versatility and relevance to various consumer needs and lifestyles. By highlighting the diverse applications of the product, marketers can attract a wider range of consumers who may find different uses for it, thereby expanding the potential market for the product.

4. Positioning based on product category. This positioning is usually done by new products that appear in a product category. Positioning based on product category is a strategy often employed when introducing new products to the market. It involves associating the product with a specific category or class of products that consumers are already familiar with. This helps consumers understand the nature and purpose of the new product quickly, leveraging the existing associations and expectations they have with the product category. By positioning the new product within a recognized category, marketers can facilitate its acceptance and adoption by consumers, as it fits into their existing mental frameworks and purchasing habits.

5. Positioning to competitors. Positioning based on competitors in modern advertising is commonplace. Positioning through imagination. Marketers can develop their product positioning by using imaginations such as places, people, objects, and situations. Positioning by comparing to competitors is a common strategy in modern advertising. This involves directly or indirectly referencing competitors to highlight the advantages

of one's own product or brand. Additionally, positioning through imagination is a creative approach where marketers use evocative imagery, associations with places, people, objects, or situations to shape consumer perception and create a distinct brand identity.

6. Problem-based positioning. Especially for new products/services that are not yet well known. New products are usually created to provide solutions to their consumers. The problems felt in society or experienced by consumers are studied further and the products offered are positioned to solve these problems. Problem-based positioning is a marketing strategy specifically designed for new or unfamiliar products and services. It centers on identifying and addressing the problems or pain points experienced by consumers. By conducting thorough research and understanding the issues faced by the target audience, companies can position their offerings as solutions to these problems. This approach not only helps in creating awareness and generating interest in the new product but also establishes its relevance and value in the market.

The main objectives of positioning analysis are: positioning and placing products in a market that shows that the product is very different from competing brands, positioning a product to be able to convey several messages to customers, achieving results as expected to fulfill a need in a specific market segment, avoiding sudden changes in sales and creating a customer confidence a brand is offered [15]. Positioning failures can bring down a company's marketing strategy [16].

Things that are included in positioning errors are as follows:

- Underpositioning, consumers have little knowledge about the company's products, making consumers feel nothing about the company's characteristics. Underpositioning refers to a scenario where consumers have limited awareness or understanding of a company's products. This lack of knowledge leads to a lack of differentiation in the minds of consumers, making the company's offerings indistinguishable from competitors.

Essentially, the company's products fail to make a lasting impression or evoke any specific feelings or associations in consumers.

- Overpositioning, consumers have too narrow knowledge and understanding of the company, product or brand. Overpositioning occurs when consumers have a very limited and narrow understanding of a company, its products, or its brand. This limited perception can restrict the brand's appeal and potential customer base. It may lead consumers to associate the brand with only a specific niche or use case, overlooking its broader capabilities or offerings.
- Confused positioning, frequent changes make consumers confused about contradictory messages about brand positioning. Confused positioning arises when a brand frequently changes its messaging or positioning strategies, leading to conflicting or contradictory information for consumers. This inconsistency can create confusion and uncertainty in the minds of consumers, making it difficult for them to form a clear and consistent understanding of the brand's identity and value proposition.

Multidimensional Scaling (MDS)

Multidimensional Scaling (MDS) is a powerful statistical technique used to simplify complex, multidimensional data into a more manageable and interpretable lower-dimensional space [17]. This simplification is achieved while preserving the essential information and relationships within the data [18]. MDS is a versatile tool in multivariate statistical analysis, primarily employed to determine the relative positions of objects based on their perceived similarities or dissimilarities [19].

One of the key applications of MDS lies in its ability to uncover the underlying dimensions that influence how individuals evaluate or perceive objects. By analyzing the patterns of similarity and dissimilarity among objects, MDS can reveal the hidden factors or attributes that shape people's judgments and preferences [5, 20]. This information is invaluable for understanding consumer behavior, market dynamics, and decision-making processes.

MDS is also widely recognized as perceptual mapping [5]. Perceptual maps are visual representations of how people perceive different brands, products, or services in relation to each other. In these maps, the distance between points representing different objects reflects their perceived similarity or dissimilarity, as measured by various variables or attributes [21]. Perceptual maps provide a valuable tool for researchers and marketers to visualize and analyze consumer perceptions, preferences, and the competitive landscape. They offer insights into how brands are positioned in the minds of consumers, which attributes are most salient, and how brands can differentiate themselves from competitors [22].

The versatility of MDS has led to its application in a wide range of fields and research areas. In environmental studies, MDS has been used for clustering and analyzing nuisance data, helping to identify patterns and sources of environmental problems [23]. In the realm of web services, MDS has been employed to cluster and categorize services based on their functional similarities, aiding in the discovery and selection of appropriate services [24].

Moreover, MDS has found applications in analyzing behavioral data from time-based games or simulations, providing insights into player behavior and preferences [25]. In the field of economics, MDS has been utilized to assess regional economic development, revealing the underlying factors that contribute to economic disparities and growth patterns [26]. Additionally, MDS has been employed in statistical modeling for variable selection strategies, helping to identify the most relevant variables for predicting outcomes [27]. Even in engineering, MDS has been applied to identify factors affecting the reliability of deep wells, contributing to improved maintenance and risk assessment [28].

SWOT Analysis

SWOT analysis is a strategic framework used to assess an organization's internal strengths and weaknesses, as well as external opportunities and threats [29, 30, 31]. It provides a structured approach to evaluating a company's current situation and its potential for future growth and success. By identifying and analyzing these factors, businesses can develop actionable strategies to leverage their strengths, address their weaknesses, capitalize on opportunities, and mitigate potential threats.

SWOT analysis is a well-established and widely used technique in business management [32]. It serves as a snapshot of a company's strategic position, offering a comprehensive overview of its internal capabilities and external environment. The analysis involves categorizing various factors into four quadrants: strengths, weaknesses, opportunities, and threats. Strengths and weaknesses are internal factors that are within the company's control, while opportunities and threats are external factors that arise from the market or broader environment.

It is important to note that SWOT analysis is primarily a descriptive tool, not a prescriptive one [33]. It helps to identify and organize relevant information about a company's situation but does not directly provide solutions to the identified problems or challenges. Instead, it serves as a foundation for further analysis and strategic planning, enabling managers to make informed decisions based on a comprehensive understanding of their company's strengths, weaknesses, opportunities, and threats.

Competitive Strategy

In the dynamic and fiercely competitive e-commerce landscape, companies must formulate robust competitive strategies to thrive and maintain their market position [11]. A competitive strategy encompasses a set of actions and initiatives that a company undertakes to attract and retain customers, outperform rivals, and achieve sustainable growth in the market [3]. It involves making deliberate choices about target markets, value propositions, and resource allocation to gain a competitive advantage [13].

E-commerce companies, like Shopee, face unique challenges and opportunities in developing their competitive strategies [1]. The digital nature of the business, the rapid pace of technological advancements, and the constantly evolving consumer preferences necessitate a flexible and adaptive approach [9]. Companies must leverage their strengths, address their weaknesses, and capitalize on emerging trends to stay ahead of the competition [6].

A successful competitive strategy in e-commerce often involves a combination of factors, including:

- **Differentiation:** Offering unique products or services that set the company apart from its competitors [14].
- **Cost leadership:** Providing products or services at a lower cost than competitors [13].
- **Focus:** Concentrating on a specific niche market or customer segment [13].
- **Innovation:** Continuously introducing new products, services, or features to attract and retain customers [9].
- **Customer experience:** Providing a seamless and enjoyable shopping experience across all touchpoints [8].

By carefully analyzing the market dynamics, understanding consumer behavior, and aligning their strategies with their core competencies, e-commerce companies can develop competitive strategies that enable them to thrive in the digital marketplace.

E-commerce Business Strategy

E-commerce, or electronic commerce, has revolutionized the way businesses operate and consumers shop [1, 2]. It encompasses a wide range of online activities, including buying and selling goods and services, online auctions, and electronic payments [7]. The growth of e-commerce has been fueled by advancements in technology, increased internet penetration, and changing consumer behavior, particularly in the wake of the COVID-19 pandemic [10].

E-commerce platforms, also known as online marketplaces, provide a virtual space where businesses and consumers can interact and transact [8]. These platforms offer various benefits, such as convenience, accessibility, wider product selection, and competitive prices [12]. However, the e-commerce landscape is highly competitive, with numerous players vying for market share [11]. To succeed in this environment, businesses need to develop effective e-commerce business strategies.

An e-commerce business strategy outlines how a company plans to leverage the online marketplace to achieve its goals [3]. It involves defining the target market, identifying the value proposition, and determining the most effective ways to reach and engage customers [13]. A well-defined e-commerce business strategy can help businesses increase their online visibility, drive traffic to their websites or online stores, and ultimately boost sales and revenue [9].

Several key components contribute to a successful e-commerce business strategy:

1. **Business Model:** Choosing the right business model is crucial for e-commerce success. Common models include business-to-consumer (B2C), where businesses sell directly to consumers; consumer-to-consumer (C2C), where consumers sell to each other through a platform; and business-to-business (B2B), where businesses sell to

other businesses [1]. Each model has its own unique characteristics and requires different strategies.

2. **Marketing Strategy:** Effective marketing is essential for attracting and retaining customers in the online marketplace [9]. E-commerce businesses utilize various digital marketing channels, such as search engine optimization (SEO), social media marketing, email marketing, and content marketing, to reach their target audience and promote their products or services [9].

3. **Operational Strategy:** Efficient operations are critical for delivering a seamless customer experience and ensuring profitability [8]. This includes managing inventory, fulfilling orders, processing payments, and providing customer support [8]. E-commerce businesses often leverage technology and automation to streamline their operations and improve efficiency.

By developing a comprehensive e-commerce business strategy that encompasses these key components, businesses can effectively navigate the complexities of the online marketplace and achieve sustainable growth.

Research Objectives And Benefits

Research Objective

The specific objectives of this research are:

1. Knowing Shopee's e-commerce positioning, based on perceptual mapping.
2. Developing strategies to win the competition based on current positioning.

Research Benefits

The benefits of this research include:

1. Provide input for Shopee or other e-commerce regarding its position in the current competition, based on consumer perceptions. By providing input for Shopee or other e-commerce platforms regarding their position in the current competition based on consumer perceptions, this research offers valuable insights into how these platforms are perceived by their target audience. This information can be used to identify areas of strength and weakness, as well as opportunities for improvement and differentiation. By understanding consumer perceptions, e-commerce platforms can tailor their strategies and offerings to better meet the

needs and preferences of their customers, ultimately leading to increased competitiveness and market share.

2. Add insight into knowledge and literature that can be used by lecturers, students, and people who are interested in studying the topic of integration of multidimensional scaling and SWOT methods. This research contributes to the existing knowledge and literature by demonstrating the practical application and effectiveness of integrating multidimensional scaling (MDS) and SWOT analysis in a real-world business context. This integration offers a comprehensive approach to understanding market positioning and developing competitive strategies. By showcasing the step-by-step process and outcomes of this integrated methodology, the research provides a valuable reference for lecturers, students, and researchers interested in exploring the synergies between these two analytical tools. It can serve as a guide for future studies and applications in various fields, including marketing, strategic management, and consumer behavior research.

Research Methodology

Research Flow

The research process begins with a comprehensive review of existing literature and initial observations to establish a solid foundation. This is followed by the identification of the core problem the research aims to address and the formulation of specific objectives to guide the study. Operational variables, which are measurable factors relevant to the research, are then defined.

Next, questionnaires are designed to collect data from a selected population or sample. The collected data is then processed using two distinct methods: multidimensional scaling (MDS) and SWOT analysis. MDS helps visualize perceptions and preferences, while SWOT evaluates internal and external factors influencing the research subject.

The processed data is then thoroughly analyzed and discussed to draw meaningful conclusions and insights. Finally, the research process culminates with the presentation of the final findings and recommendations. This systematic approach ensures a rigorous and comprehensive investigation, leading to valuable knowledge and informed decision-making.

The research process follows a systematic approach to ensure a comprehensive and rigorous investigation:

1. **Literature Review and Initial Observations:** The research begins with an extensive review of existing literature and preliminary observations related to the topic. This step aims to establish a solid foundation of knowledge and understanding, identifying key concepts, theories, and previous findings relevant to the research problem.

2. **Problem Identification and Objectives Formulation:** Based on the literature review and initial observations, the core problem that the research seeks to address is clearly defined. Specific research objectives are then formulated to guide the study and outline the desired outcomes.

3. **Operational Variables Definition:** The next step involves defining the operational variables, which are the measurable factors that will be examined in the research. These variables are carefully selected based on their relevance to the research objectives and their ability to provide meaningful insights into the problem under investigation.

4. **Questionnaire Design and Data Collection:** Questionnaires are designed to collect data from a selected population or sample. The questionnaire includes carefully crafted questions or statements that aim to capture respondents' perceptions, opinions, and preferences regarding the operational variables.

5. **Data Processing (MDS and SWOT Analysis):** The collected data is then processed using two distinct methods: multidimensional scaling (MDS) and SWOT analysis. MDS is a statistical technique that helps visualize the relationships between different variables and creates perceptual maps to understand consumer perceptions and preferences. SWOT analysis is a strategic framework that evaluates the internal strengths and weaknesses of the subject, as well as the external opportunities and threats it faces.

6. **Data Analysis and Discussion:** The processed data from both MDS and SWOT analysis are thoroughly analyzed and interpreted. This involves identifying patterns, trends, and relationships within the data, as well as comparing and contrasting the findings from both methods to gain a deeper understanding of the research problem.

7. **Conclusions and Recommendations:** Based on the data analysis and

discussion, meaningful conclusions are drawn regarding the research objectives. These conclusions summarize the key findings and insights derived from the study. Additionally, recommendations are formulated based on the conclusions, providing actionable suggestions for addressing the research problem or improving the situation under investigation.

8. **Presentation of Final Findings:** The final step of the research process involves presenting the research findings, conclusions, and recommendations to relevant stakeholders. This may include academic peers, industry professionals, or decision-makers who can benefit from the knowledge generated by the research. The presentation may take the form of a research report, academic paper, or presentation, ensuring that the findings are effectively communicated and disseminated to the appropriate audience.

Type of Research

This research is a quantitative study conducted by distributing questionnaires containing several questions for e-commerce user consumers.

This research is a quantitative study that collects data by distributing questionnaires to e-commerce users. The questionnaires contain several questions designed to gather numerical data on consumer perceptions and preferences regarding various e-commerce platforms. This quantitative approach allows for statistical analysis of the data, enabling researchers to draw objective conclusions and make informed recommendations based on the numerical findings.

Data Source

1. Literature Study. At this stage, theories and references are obtained from books and other academic sources regarding the research topic being carried out.
2. Questionnaire. The data contained in this study were collected using a

questionnaire, by providing a list of statements. Respondents were asked to respond to the questions or statements submitted. The measurement scale uses a Likert scale (1 – 5) [34].

The data collection in this research involved two main sources:

1. **Literature Study:** This stage involved gathering relevant theories, concepts, and findings from existing books, academic papers, and other credible sources related to e-commerce, positioning strategies, multidimensional scaling (MDS), and SWOT analysis. The literature review provided a theoretical foundation for the research and helped identify gaps in knowledge that the study aimed to address.

2. **Questionnaire:** A questionnaire was designed to collect primary data directly from e-commerce users. The questionnaire consisted of a series of statements related to various attributes of e-commerce platforms, such as ease of use, information quality, customer service, and price. Respondents were asked to rate their agreement or disagreement with each statement using a Likert scale ranging from 1 (strongly disagree) to 5 (strongly agree). This allowed for the quantification of consumer perceptions and preferences, enabling statistical analysis and the creation of perceptual maps using MDS.

Population and Sample

The population in this study are consumers who have made transactions or purchases through the shopee e-commerce application in Ambon city. Meanwhile, the sample is part of the number and characteristics possessed by the population. The sampling technique in this study used non-probability sampling. Non-probability sampling is a sampling technique for not providing opportunities or opportunities to members of the population selected to be sampled [35].

The stages of determining the sample include:

- Respondents have an e-commerce account.
- Respondents have made transactions at least 2 times in any e-commerce.
- Respondents live in Ambon City.

The population in this study consisted of all consumers in Ambon City who had used the Shopee e-commerce app for transactions or purchases. However, due to the large size and diversity of this population, it was not feasible to survey every individual. Therefore, a sample was selected to represent the population.

By applying these criteria, the researchers aimed to select a sample that was representative of the broader population of Shopee users in Ambon City, while also ensuring that the respondents had some experience with e-commerce transactions. This approach allowed for a more focused and efficient data collection process, while still providing valuable insights into consumer perceptions and preferences regarding Shopee and its competitors.

Attributes

The research attributes were adapted from Hasibuan, et al. [15], consisting of: 1) ease of use, 2) information quality, 3) customer service, 4) website/application design, 5) process control, 6) outcome quality, and 7) price.

The operational definitions of research attributes in the table are as follows:

1. Ease of Use: This attribute refers to the accessibility and user-friendliness of the website, including its features. Indicators used to measure this are:

- The website is easy to use.
- The features are easy to understand and utilize.
- The measurement scale for this attribute is ordinal, meaning responses are ranked in order of agreement.

2. Information Quality: This attribute pertains to the clarity and detail of information provided on the website. The indicator used is:

- The information provided by the seller on the website is clear and detailed.
- The measurement scale is ordinal.

3. Customer Service: This attribute focuses on the ability of customers to communicate with customer service regarding services and complaints. Indicators include:

- After-sales service is helpful and satisfactory.
- Customer service is responsive to complaints.
- Customer service can resolve issues effectively.
- The measurement scale is ordinal.

4. Website/Application Design: This attribute concerns the ease of access provided by the website's appearance. The indicator used is:

- The website has an attractive design.
- The measurement scale is ordinal.

5. Process Control: This attribute refers to the monitoring of the shipping process for goods purchased by consumers. The indicator used is:

- The tracking process for purchased products is easy to do.
- The measurement scale is ordinal.

6. Outcome Quality: This attribute relates to the quality of goods received by consumers. Indicators include:

- The goods received match the order.
- The goods received match the description.
- A money-back guarantee is provided if the goods delivered do not match.
- The measurement scale is ordinal.

7. Price: This attribute represents the amount of money consumers must pay to purchase a product. Indicators include:

- Lower prices.
- Product discounts.
- Free shipping costs.
- Cashback for certain product purchases.
- The measurement scale is ordinal.

Data Collection Technique

This study uses data collection techniques carried out by distributing questionnaires from google form which contains several questions for shopee e-commerce users. The type of questionnaire used in this study is a closed questionnaire by asking several questions, where the respondent chooses an alternative answer according to the respondent's choice. Likert scale is used as a form of respondent's response to questions.

Data Analysis Method

The method employed in designing Shopee's positioning strategy for e-commerce users in Ambon City is Multidimensional Scaling (MDS). To analyze the acquired data, a proximity analysis technique is utilized to measure the relationships between objects or the closeness of one object to another. Proximity can be either similarity or dissimilarity between objects, with indices r and t symbolizing the r-th and t-th objects being compared.

Consider a set of n objects with dissimilarity $\delta(r,t)$, where r,t = 1,2,...,n. A configuration of n points in a p-dimensional space represents the observed objects, with the distance between points denoted by d(r,t). Each point represents one object, with the r-th point representing the r-th object.

The analysis results in a perceptual map that illustrates Shopee's position compared to several competitors, along with the attributes that make it similar or different from them.

Researcher Composition and Division of Duties

The research was conducted by a team consisting of Dr. Alfredo Tutuhatunewa, ST., MT., from Pattimura University, specializing in Industrial Engineering. Dr. Tutuhatunewa dedicated 15 hours per week to the research project, undertaking various tasks including preliminary research, questionnaire design, data collection, data processing, data analysis, and the preparation of research reports. This comprehensive involvement ensured a thorough and systematic approach to the research, covering all stages from initial investigation to final reporting.

Results and Discussion

Marketplace Overview

Shopee

Shopee is an online buying and selling application that can be accessed easily using a smartphone that belongs to the e-commerce category. Shopee arrived in Indonesia in 2015 with the vision of "becoming the number 1 mobile marketplace in Indonesia" and the mission of "developing an entrepreneurial spirit for sellers in Indonesia", (Isparwati, n.d.). One of the strategies carried out by shopee is to use a push and pull strategy, which is a promotional strategy with advertising and campaign programs so that users are comfortable and encouraged to use shopee.

At the beginning of its establishment, Shopee launched as a consumer to consumer (C2C) marketplace. However, it has now shifted to a hybrid model of C2C and business to consumer (B2C) since launching Shopee Mall, which is an online store platform for well-known brands. Shopee is the leading online shopping platform in Southeast Asia and Taiwan, which is customized for each region and provides an easy, convenient, safe, and fast online shopping experience for customers through strong logistics and payment support.

Shopee arrived in Indonesia in 2015 with the vision of "becoming the number 1 mobile marketplace in Indonesia" and the mission of "developing an entrepreneurial spirit for sellers in Indonesia", (Isparwati, n.d.). One of the strategies carried out by shopee is to use a push and pull strategy, which is a promotional strategy with advertising and campaign programs so that users are comfortable and encouraged to use shopee.

Lazada

On March 15, 2012 the Lazada website was launched in 5 countries, namely Indonesia, Malaysia, the Philippines, Singapore, Thailand and Vietnam. The initial launch of Lazada had 4000 products for sale and was divided into 4 categories. Within a week or so of getting the first customer and giving a good assessment in terms of purchasing until after buying the product from Lazada, so that at that time Lazada got 1000 customers in the first month. The rapid growth of customers and suppliers so that in August 2012 Lazada recruited 200 employees after hard work from the beginning of the launch until August 2012.

At the end of 2012 Lazada changed the design of its website to be more enjoyed by customers and suppliers and provide convenience for people looking for products in it. Currently, Lazada's download numbers have reached 100 million downloads on the Google Play Store.

Tokopedia

In 2009 Tokopedia started a C2C marketplace business. C2C (Customer to Customer) is a business model that facilitates product or service transactions between customers. The purpose of C2C is to enable interaction relationships between customers, helping buyers and sellers find each other. Tokopedia does not facilitate payments or money processing, rather it simply facilitates a relationship, either between an item owner and a potential buyer, or someone looking for a particular service and an expert who can provide it. Currently, Shopee's download numbers have reached 50 million downloads on the Google

Play Store.

Bukalapak

In 2010 Bukalapak was founded by Achmad Zaky as CEO, Muhammad Fajrin Rasyid as CFO, Nugroho Herucahyono as CFO. After a year of running, Bukalapak began to be looked at by many investors with the Batavia Incubator company led by Takeshi Ebihara as the first investor. In 2015, Emtek Group entered through a subsidiary called PT Kreatif Media Karya. Because after many investors Bukalapak is progressing rapidly with evidence of the many awards won. The peak of the award in 2017 and 2018 was the Achmad Bakrie CVI 2018 award, Youtube Pulse 2018 and others.

Until now Bukalapak continues to develop and also innovate into a better site to meet the needs of users from all fields of business. The owners of Bukalapak now are Suitmedia and also Kreatif Media Karya while Rachmat Kaimuddin as CEO, Willix Halim as COO and also Teddy Oetomo as CSO. (Bukalapak.com). Currently, Bukalapak's download numbers have reached 50 million downloads on the Google Play Store.

Blibli

Blibli offers a wide range of products and provides the best service based on the value of Customer Satisfaction First, by providing 24-hour customer service for seven days. Blibli also prioritizes quality products guaranteed 100% original, free shipping, secure payments, installments without credit cards, fast delivery, and returns within 15 days.

Blibli also conducts online to offline (O2O) sales, an approach that blends online channels and physical stores, through the Blibli In Store and Click & Collect programs that allow consumers to shop online and offline at once. Of course, this is done as Blibli's commitment to provide a memorable online shopping experience to all its customers.

Respondent Description

This study emphasizes to determine consumer perceptions in choosing the Shopee, Lazada, Tokopedia, Bukalapak and BliBli marketplaces that have been determined by the researcher. Respondents in this study were 150 people who live in Ambon city and have used the five marketplaces.

To understand individual consumer perceptions, researchers distributed questionnaires to each respondent. Recognizing the diversity among respondents, researchers grouped them based on specific characteristics: gender, age, and occupation.

Regarding gender, out of the 150 respondents, 64 were male and 86 were female, indicating a slightly higher representation of female participants.

The distribution of respondents based on age and occupation is further detailed in subsequent tables, providing a comprehensive overview of the sample's demographic composition.The data on respondents' gender reveals that out of the total 150 participants, 64 were male and 86 were female. This distribution indicates a slightly larger proportion of female participants compared to male participants in the study.

The age distribution of respondents reveals that the majority, consisting of 85 individuals, are between 21 and 24 years old. The second largest group comprises 34 respondents aged 17 to 20. The remaining respondents are distributed across the 25-28 age range (20 individuals) and those over 28 years old (11 individuals). This data indicates a concentration of respondents in the younger age brackets, particularly between 17 and 24 years old.

The respondent data based on occupation shows that the majority of respondents are workers or students, with a total of 98 people. This is followed by students (10 people), civil servants (17 people), entrepreneurs (13 people), private employees (8 people), military/police (3 people), and unemployed (3 people).

Validity and Reliability Test Results

The validity and reliability of the research instrument were assessed using SPSS. The validity of each item was determined by comparing the calculated r-value (rhitung) with the critical r-value (rtabel). If rhitung exceeded rtabel, or if the significance level was less than 0.05, the item was considered valid.

The analysis revealed that all rhitung values ranged from 0.661 to 0.906, with a significance level of 0.00. This confirmed the validity of the questionnaire for measuring consumer perceptions of e-commerce usage in Ambon City.

Reliability was assessed to determine the trustworthiness of the data, based on the distribution of rtabel values at 5% and 1% significance levels. A variable was deemed reliable if its rhitung value exceeded 0.6. The results of this reliability test indicated that all variables met this criterion, further solidifying the reliability of the questionnaire.

Reliability Test

The reliability analysis aimed to determine the internal consistency and stability of the questionnaire's results. This was achieved by examining the intercorrelations among the items within each variable. A common method for measuring reliability is Cronbach's alpha, which assesses how closely related a set of items are as a group. A high Cronbach's alpha (typically above 0.6) indicates strong internal consistency, suggesting that the items are measuring the same underlying construct reliably.

The reliability analysis involved comparing the calculated Cronbach's alpha (rhitung) with the critical values from the r-table at 5% and 1% significance levels. If the calculated alpha exceeded the critical value, the variable was considered reliable. In this study, the results of the reliability analysis revealed that all variables had Cronbach's alpha values exceeding 0.6, indicating high internal consistency and reliability. This signifies that the questionnaire consistently measured the intended constructs across different items and respondents.

The high reliability of the questionnaire is crucial as it ensures that the results obtained are not due to chance or random error. It strengthens the confidence in the findings and their generalizability to the broader population of e-commerce users in Ambon City. The consistent measurement of the variables allows for meaningful comparisons and interpretations of the data, contributing to the overall validity and robustness of the research

The Cronbach's Alpha values, ranging from 0.614 for the outcome quality variable to 0.850 for the ease of use variable, indicate that all variables demonstrate a satisfactory level of internal consistency and reliability. This suggests that the questionnaire effectively measures the overall consumer perception of e-commerce, with each variable contributing consistently to the assessment. The higher Cronbach's Alpha for ease of use highlights its particularly strong internal consistency, indicating a high degree of agreement among the items measuring this construct.

The perceptual map

The perceptual map is constructed based on data collected from respondents, representing their perceptions of several e-commerce platforms: Shopee, Lazada, Tokopedia, BliBli, and Bukalapak. The assessment is measured based on seven attributes: ease of use, information quality, customer service, website design, process control, outcome quality, and price. This map visually depicts the relative positions of these platforms in the minds of consumers, highlighting their perceived strengths and weaknesses across the evaluated attributes.

the average consumer perceptions of various e-commerce platforms (Shopee, Lazada, Tokopedia, BliBli, and Bukalapak) across seven attributes: ease of use, information quality, customer service, website design, process control, outcome quality, and price.

Shopee is perceived as the leader (ranked 1st) with the highest average rating (4.1354), excelling particularly in ease of use (4.4975) and process control (4.2050). Lazada follows closely behind (ranked 2nd) with an average rating of 4.0235, showing strength in ease of use (4.3854) and process control (4.1250).

Bukalapak secures the 3rd position with an average rating of 4.0095, standing out in website design (4.0952). Tokopedia and BliBli are ranked 4th and 5th respectively, with Tokopedia demonstrating a higher perceived price (4.0333) and BliBli having the lowest ratings across most attributes.

Overall, the data reveals that Shopee and Lazada are perceived as the top contenders in the e-commerce market, while Bukalapak maintains a competitive position. Tokopedia and BliBli have room for improvement across various attributes to enhance their appeal to consumers.

The perceptual map illustrates the positioning of five e-commerce platforms (Shopee, Lazada, Tokopedia, BliBli, and Bukalapak) based on consumer perceptions across seven attributes: ease of use, information quality, customer service, website design, process control, outcome quality, and price.

Dimension 1 appears to represent a spectrum ranging from lower perceived quality (on the left) to higher perceived quality (on the right). Dimension 2 seems to differentiate between platforms focusing on functional aspects (bottom) versus those emphasizing experiential aspects (top).

Shopee is positioned in the upper right quadrant, indicating it is perceived as having high quality and a focus on experiential aspects, particularly excelling in ease of use and customer service.

Lazada is located in the lower left quadrant, suggesting a perception of lower quality and a focus on functional aspects.

Tokopedia and Bukalapak occupy the middle right area, indicating a balance between quality and functionality, with Tokopedia leaning slightly more towards functional aspects and Bukalapak towards experiential ones.

BliBli is positioned in the lower middle area, suggesting a perception of moderate quality with a relatively balanced focus on functional and experiential aspects.

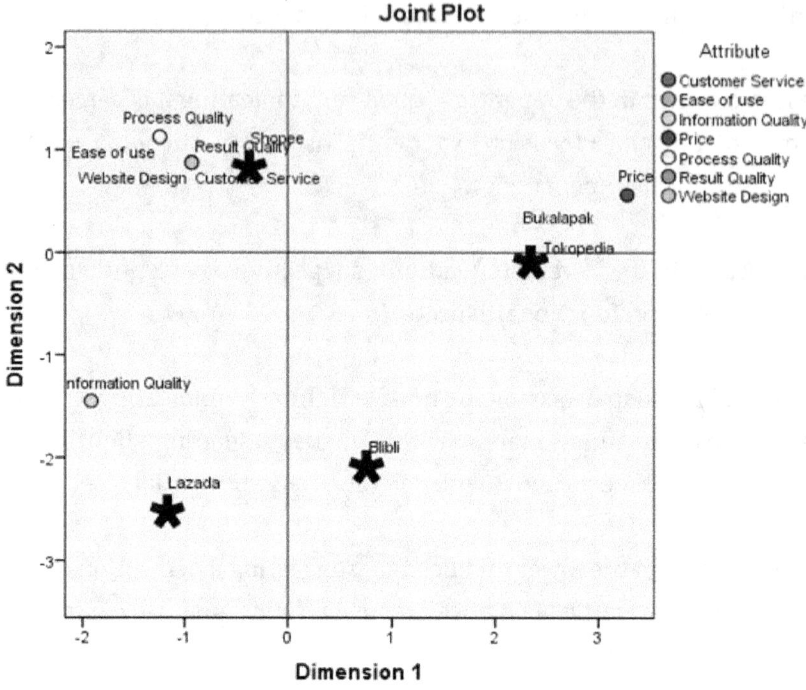

Figure 2 Perceptual Map of E-commerce Consumers in Ambon City

The attributes themselves are scattered around the map, indicating their relative importance in shaping consumer perceptions. "Ease of use" and "customer service" are positioned close to Shopee, highlighting their significance for this platform. "Information quality" is closer to Lazada, suggesting it might be a differentiating factor for this platform.

Overall, the perceptual map provides a visual representation of how consumers perceive and differentiate between these e-commerce platforms based on various attributes. This information can be valuable for companies in understanding their market position and developing targeted strategies.

The perceptual map reveals distinct positions among the five e-commerce platforms studied, based on the measured attributes. Shopee occupies a unique position in area A, indicating a distinct perception compared to other platforms. This distinctiveness is driven by attributes such as ease of use, process control, outcome quality, website design, and customer service, where Shopee excels.

Bukalapak, Tokopedia, and BliBli cluster together in area B, suggesting a perceived similarity among them. These platforms may not have a strong differentiating factor in the eyes of consumers, sharing similar strengths and weaknesses across the evaluated attributes.

Lazada stands out in area C, indicating a differentiated perception from other platforms. Its unique strength lies in the perceived quality of information it provides.

Interestingly, the attribute of price occupies a separate dimension from other attributes and e-commerce platforms. While Tokopedia and Bukalapak are perceived to have a price advantage, this attribute does not significantly influence their overall positioning on the map.

In conclusion, Shopee distinguishes itself through a combination of attributes related to user experience and product quality. Lazada differentiates through information quality, while Bukalapak, Tokopedia, and BliBli share a similar perceived profile. Price, although a potential advantage for some platforms, does not play a defining role in overall consumer perception.

SWOT Analysis

A SWOT matrix was designed to identify the strengths, weaknesses, opportunities, and threats related to the attributes that serve as recommendations for improvement for Shopee to remain competitive against its rivals. Strengths and weaknesses are internal factors within Shopee, while opportunities and threats are external factors that can influence Shopee. The attributes that serve as recommendations for improvement in the analysis of strengths, weaknesses, opportunities, and threats form the basis for creating the SWOT matrix.

1. Strengths

Based on the previous MDS analysis, Shopee's application has several strengths, including:

Ease of Use: Shopee is considered to have a user-friendly interface compared to other e-commerce applications.

Website Design: Shopee is also viewed as having an attractive web design, which is a strength in its competition with other e-commerce platforms.

Customer Service: Shopee has responsive customer service that can quickly resolve customer complaints.

Process Control: Shopee's application is considered to have ease of process control. Consumers can easily monitor the movement of goods they have ordered.

Outcome Quality: The MDS analysis also positions Shopee as an e-commerce platform capable of delivering quality goods to consumers.

2. Weaknesses

Price: Price is one of Shopee's weaknesses, but it also presents an opportunity because, on the perceptual map, price is in a different dimension from all other e-commerce platforms.

Information Quality: From the MDS analysis on the perceptual map, the quality of information provided by Shopee is not as good as the quality of information provided by Lazada.

3. Opportunities

Price: The position of the price attribute in a different dimension from all other e-commerce platforms presents an opportunity to win the competition. Shopee's ability to lower the selling price of its products will certainly greatly influence consumer choices.

Information Quality: Shopee must be able to develop its application, ensuring that the quality of information provided is accurate.

Interactive Website: Developments in information and communication technology have enabled the creation of interactive websites that are increasingly attractive to consumers across all age segments and interests.

4. Threats

Information Quality: The ability of e-commerce platforms to ensure the accuracy of information provided by partners in their product descriptions is an important factor that influences consumer perceptions of e-commerce. In this aspect, Lazada has an advantage over Shopee, based on consumer perceptions on the perceptual map.

Hacking: Hacking of applications is a threat to all application owners, including Shopee.

Entry of New Competitors: Various conveniences have been gained as a result of developments in information and communication technology, which facilitate the entry of new competitors in the e-commerce competition.

SWOT (Strengths, Weaknesses, Opportunities, and Threats) matrix for Shopee, outlining strategies to leverage strengths, address weaknesses, exploit opportunities, and mitigate threats.

SO (Strengths-Opportunities) Strategies

Enhance partnerships with vendors to ensure the lowest prices and increase promotions to attract consumers. This strategy leverages Shopee's strength in ease of use and process control, combined with the opportunity to offer the most competitive prices, to further solidify its market position.

Develop a more interactive web design to enhance the ease of use attribute, which is currently a strength for Shopee. This strategy capitalizes on Shopee's existing strength in website design and user experience to attract and retain customers in an increasingly competitive market.

Ensure the accuracy of information shared on the Shopee app to catch up with Lazada in terms of information quality. This strategy addresses Shopee's weakness in information quality by leveraging its strengths in other areas, such as process control and customer service, to build trust and credibility with consumers.

WO (Weaknesses-Opportunities) Strategies

Increase joint promotional programs with seller partners to obtain the lowest prices for consumers. This strategy aims to overcome Shopee's weakness in price by collaborating with sellers to offer attractive deals and discounts, thereby attracting price-sensitive consumers.

Continuously strive to improve the quality of information shared on the app and website through collaboration with seller partners. This strategy addresses the weakness in information quality by working closely with sellers to ensure accurate and reliable product information, enhancing the overall shopping experience.

ST (Strengths-Threats) Strategies

Continuously strive to improve the quality of information shared on the app and website through collaboration with seller partners. This strategy aims to mitigate the threat posed by Lazada's superior information quality by actively working with sellers to enhance the accuracy and reliability of product information on Shopee's platform.

Increase the security level of the application to ensure it is safe from hacking threats. This strategy addresses the threat of hacking by proactively implementing robust security measures to protect user data and maintain the platform's integrity.

Ensure that all strengths are maintained to compete with the entry of new competitors. This strategy focuses on preserving Shopee's existing strengths, such as ease of use, customer service, and process control, to maintain a competitive edge in the face of new entrants in the market.

WT (Weaknesses-Threats) Strategies

Continuously strive to improve the quality of information shared on the app and website through collaboration with seller partners. This strategy aims to address both the weakness in information quality and the threat posed by Lazada's superior information in this area by actively working with sellers to enhance the accuracy and reliability of product information.

Reduce selling prices through collaboration with sellers and promotional programs. This strategy aims to mitigate the threat of new competitors by offering competitive prices and attractive promotions, thereby retaining existing customers and attracting new ones.

Closing

Conclusion

Based on the results of the analysis that has been carried out on the wear rate of zinc anodes and their correlation with corrosion rates in nine vessels, the following conclusions can be drawn:

1. Shopee is in a different position and dimension when compared to 5 other e-commerce on the perception map. Shopee's position is supported by the attributes of ease of use, controllable process, quality of results, website design and customer service, as Shopee's main advantages.
2. There are two main strategies that Shopee must carry out if it wants to win the competition with other e-commerce, namely cooperation with seller partners to hold promotions to reduce prices, and at the same time increase cooperation and supervision to partners, to ensure the quality of information shared on the Shopee web.

This unique positioning, supported by positive consumer perceptions of these key attributes, gives Shopee a competitive edge in the market. However, to maintain and further enhance its position, Shopee needs to implement a dual strategy. First, it should strengthen its collaboration with seller partners to offer promotions and discounts, effectively reducing prices for consumers.

Second, Shopee must simultaneously enhance cooperation and oversight with its partners to ensure the accuracy and reliability of the information shared on its platform. This two-pronged approach will not only attract price-conscious consumers but also build trust and credibility by guaranteeing the quality of information available on the Shopee website.

Suggestions

The suggestions that can be given are:

1. Shopee needs to continue to maintain the attributes that are its advantages, so that it can survive in competition with other e-commerce.
2. Further research is directed to include other attributes to complete this research analysis.

To ensure continued success and competitiveness, Shopee should prioritize maintaining and enhancing the attributes that have been identified as its key strengths, such as ease of use, process control, outcome quality, website design, and customer service. These attributes have contributed significantly to Shopee's favorable position in the market and should be consistently reinforced to retain and attract customers.

Furthermore, future research should expand the scope of analysis by incorporating additional attributes that may influence consumer perceptions and preferences in the e-commerce landscape. This could include factors such as product variety, delivery speed, return policies, and promotional activities. By considering a wider range of attributes, researchers can gain a more comprehensive understanding of the factors that drive consumer choices and develop more targeted recommendations for e-commerce platforms to improve their competitiveness.

References

[1] V. Jain, B. Malviya, and S. Arya, "An Overview of Electronic Commerce (e-Commerce)," *cibg*, vol. 27, no. 3, Apr. 2021, doi: 10.47750/cibg.2021.27.03.090.

[2] A. Gupta, "E-COMMERCE: ROLE OF E-COMMERCE IN TODAY'S BUSINESS," *International Journal of Computing and Corporate Research*, vol. 4, no. 1, 2014.

[3] P. Kotler and G. Armstrong, *Principles of Marketing.* in The Prentice-Hall series in marketing. Pearson, 2010. [Online]. Available: https://books.google.co.id/books?id=ZW2u5LOmbs4C

[4] A. Hasan, *Marketing.* Yogyakarta: Media Utama, 2008.

[5] J. F. Hair, W. C. Black, B. J. Babin, and R. E. Anderson, *Multivariate Data Analysis.* Pearson Education Limited, 2013.

[6] W. S. G. R. Devi, D. R. Pringgandinie, H. Yulina, and D. Hadiansah, "SWOT Analysis as A Competitive Strategy at Primkop Kartika Ardagusema Cimahi City, West Java, Indonesia," *IJSTM*, vol. 3, no. 1, pp. 134–143, Jan. 2022, doi: 10.46729/ijstm.v3i1.451.

[7] M. Mariana, "Apa itu E-Commerce," Universitas Pasundan. Accessed: Apr. 03, 2023. [Online]. Available: https://www.unpas.ac.id/apa-itu-e-commerce/

[8] E. Turban, D. King, J. K. Lee, T.-P. Liang, and D. C. Turban, *Electronic Commerce: A Managerial and Social Networks Perspective.* in Springer Texts in Business and Economics. Cham: Springer International Publishing, 2015. doi: 10.1007/978-3-319-10091-3.

[9] A. Rosário and R. Raimundo, "Consumer Marketing Strategy and E-Commerce in the Last Decade: A Literature Review," *Journal of Theoretical and Applied Electronic Commerce Research*, vol. 16, no. 7, Art. no. 7, Dec. 2021, doi: 10.3390/jtaer16070164.

[10] T. Kawasaki, H. Wakashima, and R. Shibasaki, "The use of e-commerce and the COVID-19 outbreak: A panel data analysis in Japan," *Transport Policy*, vol. 115, pp. 88–100, Jan. 2022, doi: 10.1016/j.tranpol.2021.10.023.

[11] V. Babenko, Z. Kulczyk, I. Perevosova, O. Syniavska, and O. Davydova, "Factors of the development of international e-commerce under the conditions of globalization," *SHS Web Conf.*, vol. 65, p. 04016, 2019, doi: 10.1051/shsconf/20196504016.

[12] R. Kalakota and A. B. Whinston, *Electronic Commerce: A Manager's Guide.* Addison-Wesley Professional, 1997.

[13] P. Kotler and K. L. Keller, *Marketing Management*, 13th ed. Pearson Prentice Hall, 2009.

[14] R. Kasali, *Membidik Pasar Indonesia: Segmentasi, Targeting, Positioning.* Jakarta: Gramedia Pustaka Utama, 2007.

[15] A. N. Hasibuan, O. Suharli, and R. Andriyanty, "ANALISIS POSITION-ING PEMETAAN MARKETPLACE BERDASARKAN PERSEPSI KONSUMEN DI JAKARTA SELATAN," *Jurnal Ekobis: Ekonomi Bisnis & Manajemen*, vol. 12, no. 1, Art. no. 1, Apr. 2022, doi: 10.37932/j.e.v12i1.446.

[16] D. W. Cravens and N. Piercy, *Strategic Marketing*. McGraw-Hill Irwin, 2009.

[17] E. Peterfreund and M. Gavish, "Multidimensional scaling of noisy high dimensional data," *Applied and Computational Harmonic Analysis*, vol. 51, pp. 333–373, Mar. 2021, doi: 10.1016/j.acha.2020.11.006.

[18] N. Saeed, H. Nam, T. Y. Al-Naffouri, and M.-S. Alouini, "A State-of-the-Art Survey on Multidimensional Scaling-Based Localization Techniques," *IEEE Communications Surveys & Tutorials*, vol. 21, no. 4, pp. 3565–3583, 2019, doi: 10.1109/COMST.2019.2921972.

[19] S. Wang, "Wireless Network Indoor Positioning Method Using Nonmetric Multidimensional Scaling and RSSI in the Internet of Things Environment," *Mathematical Problems in Engineering*, vol. 2020, p. e8830891, Nov. 2020, doi: 10.1155/2020/8830891.

[20] Z. Zhang and Y. Takane, "Multidimensional Scaling," in *International Encyclopedia of Education (Third Edition)*, P. Peterson, E. Baker, and B. McGaw, Eds., Oxford: Elsevier, 2010, pp. 304–311. doi: 10.1016/B978-0-08-044894-7.01348-8.

[21] I. Gigauri, "Applying Perceptual Mapping Method for Successful Positioning Strategy," vol. 1, pp. 14–24, May 2019, doi: 10.63105/ijmbs.2019.1.1.7.

[22] A. Nigam and R. Kaushik, "Attribute Based Perceptual Mapping of Prepaid Mobile Cellular Operators: An Empirical Investigation Among Management Graduates in Central Haryana," vol. 11, 2011.

[23] A. Little, Y. Xie, and Q. Sun, "An analysis of classical multidimensional scaling with applications to clustering," *Information and Inference: A Journal of the IMA*, vol. 12, no. 1, pp. 72–112, Mar. 2023, doi: 10.1093/imaiai/iaac004.

[24] C. Shan and Y. Du, "A Web Service Clustering Method Based on Semantic

Similarity and Multidimensional Scaling Analysis," *Scientific Programming*, vol. 2021, p. e6661035, May 2021, doi: 10.1155/2021/6661035.

[25] G. Knezek, D. Gibson, R. Christensen, O. Trevisan, and M. Carter, "Assessing approaches to learning with nonparametric multidimensional scaling," *British Journal of Educational Technology*, vol. 54, no. 1, pp. 126–141, 2023, doi: 10.1111/bjet.13275.

[26] P. Hryhoruk, N. Khrushch, and S. Grygoruk, "Using Multidimensional Scaling for Assessment Economic Development of Regions," *IJIEPR*, vol. 31, no. 4, Nov. 2020, doi: 10.22068/ijiepr.31.4.597.

[27] L. Lin and D. K. H. Fong, "Bayesian multidimensional scaling procedure with variable selection," *Computational Statistics & Data Analysis*, vol. 129, pp. 1–13, Jan. 2019, doi: 10.1016/j.csda.2018.07.007.

[28] E. Kozłowski, D. Mazurkiewicz, B. Kowalska, and D. Kowalski, "Application of a Multidimensional Scaling Method to Identify the Factors Influencing on Reliability of Deep Wells," in *Intelligent Systems in Production Engineering and Maintenance*, A. Burduk, E. Chlebus, T. Nowakowski, and A. Tubis, Eds., in Advances in Intelligent Systems and Computing. Cham: Springer International Publishing, 2019, pp. 56–65. doi: 10.1007/978-3-319-97490-3_6.

[29] L. E. Quezada, E. A. Reinao, P. I. Palominos, and A. M. Oddershede, "Measuring Performance Using SWOT Analysis and Balanced Scorecard," *Procedia Manufacturing*, vol. 39, pp. 786–793, Jan. 2019, doi: 10.1016/j.promfg.2020.01.430.

[30] R. Madurai Elavarasan, S. Afridhis, R. R. Vijayaraghavan, U. Subramaniam, and M. Nurunnabi, "SWOT analysis: A framework for comprehensive evaluation of drivers and barriers for renewable energy development in significant countries," *Energy Reports*, vol. 6, pp. 1838–1864, Nov. 2020,

doi: 10.1016/j.egyr.2020.07.007.

[31] C. Namugenyi, S. L. Nimmagadda, and T. Reiners, "Design of a SWOT Analysis Model and its Evaluation in Diverse Digital Business Ecosystem Contexts," *Procedia Computer Science*, vol. 159, pp. 1145–1154, Jan. 2019, doi: 10.1016/j.procs.2019.09.283.

[32] C. E. Putri, "Analisis Strategi Bisnis Pada PT. Omega Internusa Sidoarjo," *Agora*, vol. 5, no. 1, p. 57198, 2017.

[33] F. Rangkuti, *Analisis SWOT Teknik Membedah Kasus Bisnis*. Jakarta: PT. Gramedia Pustaka Utama, 2009.

[34] R. W. Emerson, "Likert scales.," *Journal of Visual Impairment & Blindness*, vol. 111, no. 5, pp. 488–489, Sep. 2017.

[35] P. D. Sugiyono, *Metode Penelitian Bisnis*, 15th ed. Bandung: Penerbit Alfabeta, 2012.

About the Author

Dr. Alfredo Tutuhatunewa, ST., MT., is a lecturer at the Faculty of Engineering, Pattimura University, Ambon, Indonesia. He holds a doctorate in Mechanical Engineering from Brawijaya University, Malang, Indonesia. His research interests cover many topics, including supply chain management, quality management, and decision support systems. He has also researched the application of fuzzy logic in organoleptic tests and the development of business strategies using the fuzzy-SWOT method.

Dr. Tutuhatunewa focuses on supply chain analysis and improvement, particularly in the fishing and shipbuilding industries. He has developed the agile supply chain model and the SCOR model to assess and improve supply chain performance. Additionally, his research has investigated employee performance measurement and the design of performance measurement instruments using BARS and AHP methods.

Dr. Tutuhatunewa's work has been disseminated through various channels, including national and international journals and conferences. He has published articles in reputable journals such as Advances in Systems Science and Applications (ASSA), the International Journal on Engineering Applications (IREA), and Jurnal Teknik Industri. He has also presented his work at conferences such as the International Conference on Basic Science (ICBS) and the ALE National Seminar.

Furthermore, Dr. Tutuhatunewa has obtained intellectual property rights for his work, including an article on the agile supply chain model in the fishing industry in Ambon City.